MAT MAN

SHAPES

By Jan Z. Olsen • Illustrations by Molly Delaney

GET SET FOR SCHOOL™

Handwriting Without Tears®
Jan Z. Olsen, OTR

8001 MacArthur Blvd
Cabin John, MD 20818
Tel: 301-263-2700 • Fax: 301-263-2707
www.getsetforschool.com • JanOlsen@hwtears.com

Manufactured in China

First Edition
ISBN: 978-1-891627-92-7
3456789REGAL090807

If we made Mat Man with a **rectangle** ☐
What would Mat Man do?

He'd be the real Mat Man
And his mat would be blue.

If we made Mat Man with a **circle** ◯

What would Mat Man do?

He'd roll and roll
around the floor.

Then he'd roll
right out the door.

If we made Mat Man with a **diamond**

What would Mat Man do?

He'd float up high into the sky.
Then he'd look down and wave bye, bye.

If we made Mat Man with a **triangle**

What would Mat Man do?

He'd hold the triangle in his hand
Then ding-ding-ding in a marching band.

If we made Mat Man with an **oval**

What would Mat Man do?

He'd sit with Humpty on the wall

Then hold him so he wouldn't fall.

If we made Mat Man with a **moon**

What would Mat Man do?

He'd go outside to tell the cow,

"Ready! Set!
Jump over me now!"

If we made Mat Man with a **square** ☐

What would Mat Man do?

He'd take a partner
         to a dance

And do-si-do
         at every chance.

If we made Mat Man with an **octagon**

What would Mat Man do?

He'd stand in the
street like a traffic cop.

He'd make the
cars and buses stop.

If we made Mat Man with a **hexagon**

What would Mat Man do?

He'd count his sides from one to six
And then he'd stoop to pick up sticks.

If we made Mat Man with a **star**

What would Mat Man do?

He would make your wish come true,
One special wish – just for you.

If we made Mat Man with a **pentagon**

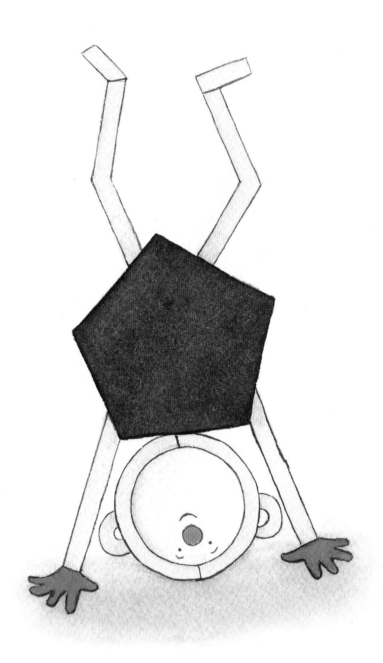

What would Mat Man do?

He'd say, "Count my fingers. Look alive!
Now count my corners up to five."

If we made Mat Man with a **heart**

What would Mat Man do?

He'd give us each a Valentine

And say, "I love you, please be mine!"

If we made Mat Man with a **blue rectangle**

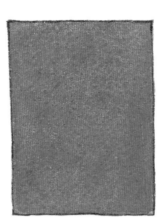

What would Mat Man do?

He'd say, " That's my mat!

My mat's bright blue!
Shapes are fun to do with you."

PLAYFUL LEARNING WITH MAT MAN™

THE ORIGINAL

Build Mat Man on your own and take him on shape adventures. This is the original Mat Man from the Get Set for School™ program. He is built with a blue rectangle mat and the capital letter wood pieces set.

MORE THAN JUST A RECTANGLE

The blue rectangle mat is just the beginning. On these pages there are guides for cutting out the other shapes in the book. Colored bottle caps are great for the eyes and nose. There is a pattern for his hands on the last page.

MAKING SHAPES

You'll need a ruler/yard stick, pencil, scissors, and color poster boards (or have children paint on white paper).

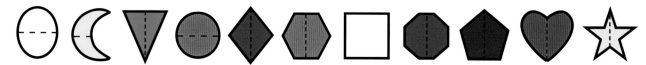

Use the grids to get the starting size right. Then cut free hand. With some of the more complicated shapes, it helps to fold the paper, draw the outline, and then cut. Laminate the shapes if you like.

STORIES AND NURSERY RHYMES

With an assortment of shapes, let the rhymes and stories flow. Have the children take turns switching the shapes. Encourage them to tell stories or say a nursery rhyme about Mat Man's new shape.

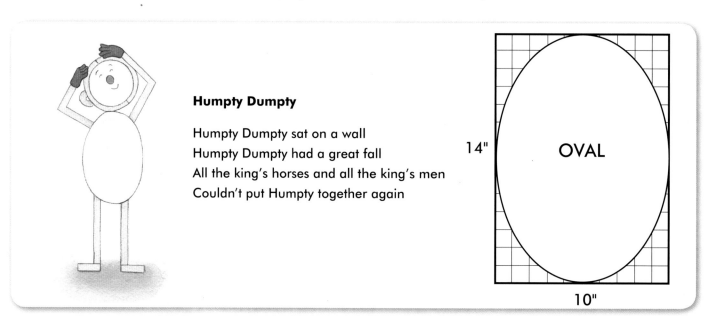

Humpty Dumpty

Humpty Dumpty sat on a wall
Humpty Dumpty had a great fall
All the king's horses and all the king's men
Couldn't put Humpty together again

14"

OVAL

10"

PLAYFUL LEARNING: SHAPES AND RHYMES

Hey, Diddle, Diddle, The Cat and The Fiddle

Hey, diddle, diddle, the cat and the fiddle
The cow jumped over the moon
The little dog laughed to see such sport
And the dish ran away with the spoon

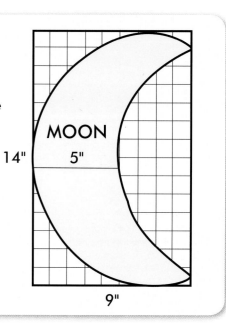

MOON
14"
5"
9"

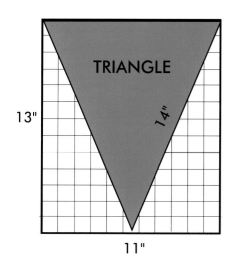

TRIANGLE
14"
13"
11"

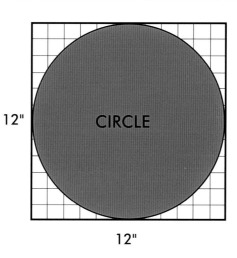

CIRCLE
12"
12"

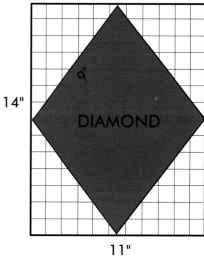

DIAMOND
9"
14"
11"

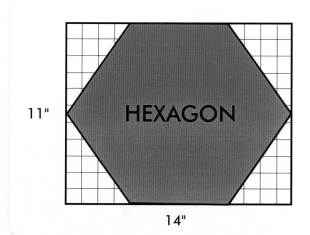

HEXAGON
11"
14"

One, Two, Buckle My Shoe

1, 2, Buckle my shoe
3, 4, Knock at the door
5, 6, Pick up sticks
7, 8, Lay them straight
9, 10, A big fat hen

PLAYFUL LEARNING: SHAPES AND RHYMES

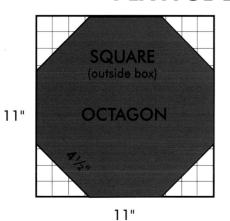

SQUARE (outside box)

OCTAGON

11"

11"

4½"

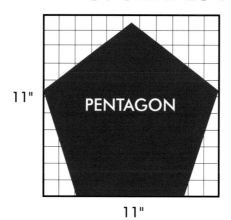

PENTAGON

11"

11"

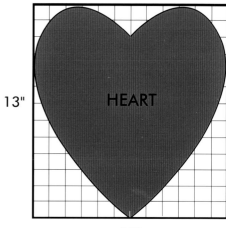

HEART

13"

12"

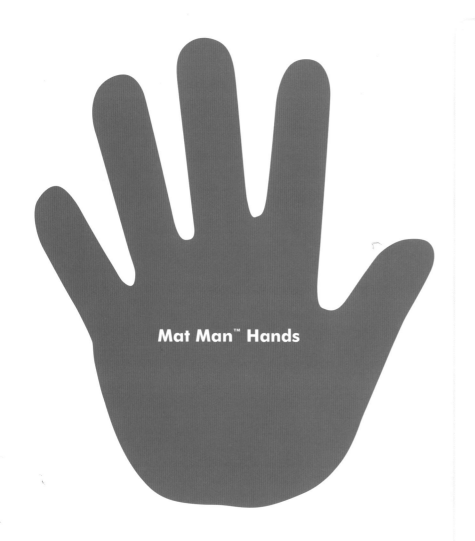

Mat Man™ Hands

Star Light, Star Bright

Star light, star bright
First star I see tonight
I wish I may, I wish I might
Have the wish, I wish tonight

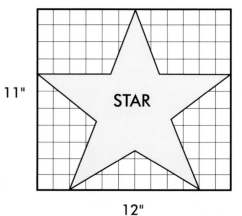

STAR

11"

12"